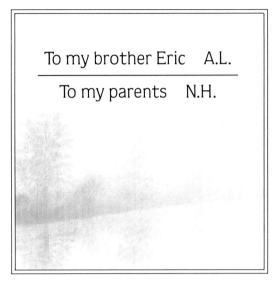

To my brother Eric   A.L.

To my parents   N.H.

First published 1983 by
Methuen Children's Books Ltd,
11 New Fetter Lane, London EC4P 4EE
in association with
Walker Books, 17-19 Hanway House,
Hanway Place, London W1P 9DL

Text © 1983 Alfred Leutscher
Illustrations © 1983 Nick Hardcastle

First printed 1983
Printed and bound by
L.E.G.O., Vicenza, Italy

British Library Cataloguing in Publication Data
Leutscher, Alfred
    Water.–(The Elements; 4)
    1. Water – Juvenile literature
    I. Title   II. Series
    553.7   TD348

ISBN 0-416-06460-4

WATER

By ALFRED LEUTSCHER

Illustrated by NICK HARDCASTLE

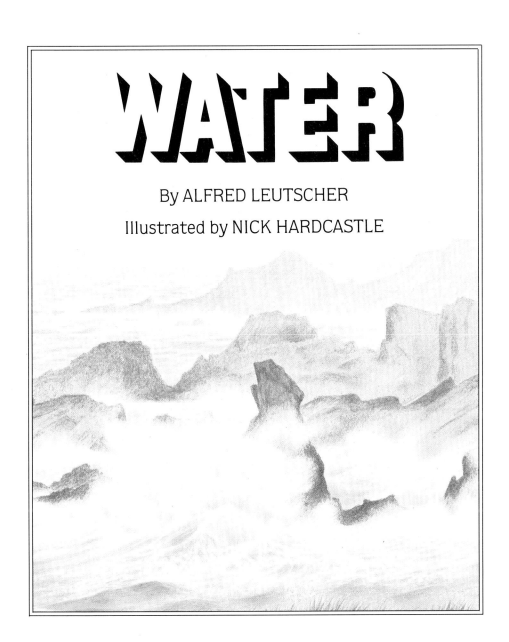

METHUEN/WALKER BOOKS

It is raining. On go our raincoats and up go the umbrellas. Mind those puddles! Water has more than one form. It is always in the air as water vapour, even though you cannot see it. When the air cannot hold any more, the vapour turns into tiny droplets that form clouds. The droplets grow, and fall as raindrops, running down our windows. Water falls on plants and animals. Every living thing needs water to grow. We cannot survive without it.

When the temperature changes water changes its form. It can freeze to become ice or boil to become steam. Water vapour from a lake rises and mixes with the air. This is called evaporation. At night, air cools. The vapour becomes tiny water droplets called dew. You can see dew on plants and spiders' webs in the morning.

In winter, the lake freezes. Icicles hang from the jetty where water once dripped. Snow falls instead of rain. Snow crystals form in clouds where the temperature is below freezing. The crystals stick together to make snowflakes. When the weather warms again, snow and ice will change back to water.

Rain falls from a cloud over a mountain. Water has no shape of its own, so tiny trickles run between rocks. Downhill, they join to form a stream, then a river. It tumbles over rocks, getting bigger and bigger until it reaches the sea. Running water wears away the earth and carves out a valley. Rocks and stones break off, are ground up and washed downstream. Sand on a beach may have come from an inland mountain. A whole mountain can be washed away by the power of water.

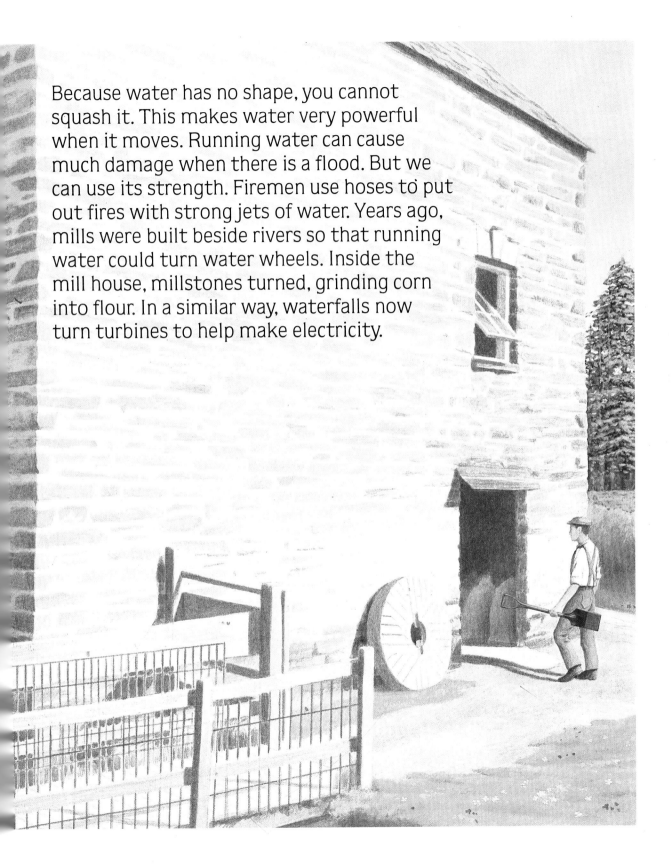

Because water has no shape, you cannot squash it. This makes water very powerful when it moves. Running water can cause much damage when there is a flood. But we can use its strength. Firemen use hoses to put out fires with strong jets of water. Years ago, mills were built beside rivers so that running water could turn water wheels. Inside the mill house, millstones turned, grinding corn into flour. In a similar way, waterfalls now turn turbines to help make electricity.

Deep inside the forest there is a splash as a tree falls into the river. It has been cut down by a beaver. With sharp teeth, the beaver nibbles off branches and adds them to a pile that stretches across the river. The beavers are building a dam. This will hold back the river so that water will rise to cover their home, called a lodge. Inside, the beavers are safe from their enemies. People build dams across rivers so that valleys fill with water. These reservoirs hold our drinking water.

It has been raining for days. As water
runs into the river, its level rises. Finally,
the river bursts its banks and floods.
This can be serious in low-lying places,
such as valleys and flat ground. Homes and
farms are cut off. In bad floods, buildings
are destroyed. Farm animals, even people,
may drown. Crops are ruined. Boats bring
food to isolated houses and rescue people.
Floods were common once. Today, most
river-banks are raised to contain the water.

The sound of falling water can be a gentle drip from a tap or a tremendous roar from a waterfall. A waterfall is where a river pours over a cliff on its way downstream. The great Victoria Falls is in Zimbabwe, southern Africa. In neighbouring Zambia, Victoria Falls is called 'Musi-oa-Tunya', which means 'smoke that thunders'. Crashing down 100 metres, the water throws up a misty spray. Sunlight shining on the spray is broken into its seven colours, which we see as a rainbow.

At the coastguard station the red flag is up. On the radio the weatherman is warning ships at sea. A storm is approaching. As it reaches the coast, huge waves smash against the cliffs, sending up clouds of spray. Pieces of rock break off, changing the shape of the coastline. At sea, a ship in distress sends a radio call for help before it hits the rocks. The cruel sea will break it up, but a helicopter arrives to save the crew.

At the North Pole, Arctic winters are long and bitter. The sea freezes into ice many metres thick. Only during the short summers, when the ice breaks up, can ships find a way through the water. This ship is stuck between sheets of floating ice, called ice floes. It is exploring the Arctic, where polar bears, seals and sea birds live. They depend on fishes that live in the water under the ice for their food. Without water, the fishes and other polar animals would die.

Plants are everywhere. Mosses, ferns, flowers and trees are all crowded together with hardly a space between. This is a tropical rain forest, warm and dripping with water. Heavy rain showers soak everything, making it easy for plants to draw up water through their roots. In dry places such as deserts, plants and animals have had to develop ways to store water. In a rain forest, where there is plenty of water and food, animals such as the crocodile find life much easier.

Life may have begun in the shallow waters of warm seas, millions of years ago. Today, seashores, rock pools and coral reefs teem with life. Brightly coloured fishes dart round the skin diver exploring the coral reef. Coral is like a skeleton, built by millions of tiny sea animals that live within it. Sea anemones, snails, sea-worms, sea urchins and starfishes are some of the animals that live on it. They all depend on water for their existence.

Like all whales, this right whale rises to the surface to breathe, before diving to the depths of the water. Hunted by people, right whales are now rare, and many other whales are endangered. Four-fifths of our planet is covered by seas. They swarm with life, from the microscopic plants to the huge whales. Yet people pollute the seas with oil and sewage. We must look after our water. Without it, there would be no life on earth.

CAMDEAN SCHOOL,
ROSYTH.